*S*harks are remarkably different from other fish. Their skeleton is made of cartilage instead of bone. Their skin is covered with raspy, toothlike scales. And contrary to popular belief, the vast majority of sharks are perfectly harmless to humans. In fact, some sharks are considered gourmet fare by seafood fanciers.

*T*he whale shark is the largest fish in the sea,
possibly reaching as much as 60 feet
in length. It could easily swallow this diver
in its cavernous mouth, yet the whale shark,
like its namesake, peacefully feeds by straining
tiny organisms from the water.

*T*he ultimate challenge between humans and beasts lies not on land, in our element, but in the sea. The ocean is the unquestioned domain of the great white shark, a predator so powerful that it could easily bite a diver in half with one snap of its mighty jaws.

SHARKS
Shorelines of America

THE STORY BEHIND THE SCENERY®

by Peter C. Howorth

Peter C. Howorth is the director of a nonprofit clinic for sick and injured marine mammals. He enjoys returning the animals to the sea with their health restored far more than he once enjoyed collecting them for oceanariums. An accomplished writer and photographer, Peter is the author of *Channel Islands: The Story Behind the Scenery*, and *Whales-Dolphins-Porpoises of the Pacific*.

Front cover: Great white shark, photo by Marty Snyderman. Inside front cover: Silhouette of an oceanic white-tipped shark, photo by Al Giddings-Ocean Images. Page 1: Diver with Pacific angel shark. Pages 2/3: Diver with whale shark. Page 4: Diver Chip Matheson filming great white shark. Photos by Marty Snyderman. Page 5: Whitetip reef shark, photo by Tom Campbell.

Edited by Mary L. Van Camp. Book design by K. C. DenDooven.

Second Printing, 1992
SHARKS: SHORELINES OF AMERICA. © 1991 KC PUBLICATIONS, INC.
LC 91-60038. ISBN 0-88714-063-7.

SHARK is a household word, yet few people know anything about the shark itself. Many fanciful tales are told about it, and these yarns gain wide acceptance even though they are seldom true.

The shark has been called a mindless machine of destruction—the perfect killer. Actually, like many top-level predators, it can be rather sloppy and sometimes just wounds its prey, allowing it to escape. Even when it does make a kill, it frequently does not eat all of it, especially if the prey is large.

The shark is said to have an insatiable appetite, but evidence suggests it has no appetite at all, in the way that we understand it. Its feeding impulse is probably triggered by its senses instead of by a growling stomach, and its senses are so refined and different from ours as to nearly defy description.

Many people claim the shark is primitive, if only because it has remained essentially unchanged for hundreds of millions of years. But the shark has had little need to change—it is a supremely well-adapted predator. Over 200 species of sharks thrive from the deepest abyss to the shallowest lagoon, from the polar

The ubiquitous blue shark has acquired a largely undeserved reputation as a killer. In reality, the blue prefers prey much smaller than itself. Squid, mackerel and other small schooling fish form the bulk of its diet. The blue will occasionally feed on larger prey, but only when the prey is wounded or dead. Divers who spear fish, or photographers who "chum" with cut-up fish, attract blue sharks with the promise of food. This can prove dangerous.

The oceanic whitetip shark is an open-water species found throughout the warmer regions of the Pacific. It is an eminently capable predator. This shark has attacked victims of airplane crashes and shipwrecks, and has a well-deserved reputation for ferocity. Fortunately, it swims well offshore and is rarely seen by humans.

seas to the sunlit tropics, with at least one species inhabiting lakes and rivers.

On the West Coast of the United States, about 40 types are found, ranging from the huge but harmless whale shark to the well-named pygmy shark. Many of the open water species are also found off Hawaii, along with various types of tropical reef sharks. Most sharks pose no threat to humans, but the great white shark is a notable exception. More people have been attacked by great whites in California than in any other part of the world.

Evolution of a Supreme Predator

Some 300 million years ago, a strange fish swam the primordial seas of what is now the south shore of Lake Erie, near Cleveland, Ohio. This fish probably came from a different lineage than the others, because it had cartilage instead of bone. It was dubbed *Cladoselache*, and it was the earliest known shark.

This prehistoric fish had a spine in front of each of its two dorsal fins—possibly to discourage predators—a broad, symmetrical tail, and stiff, triangular pectoral fins. Unlike nearly all modern sharks, its jaws were at the end of its snout.

More than 100 million years later, the first ancestor of one of today's sharks appeared. It looked very similar to the spiny dogfish, which is actually a shark. By the end of the Cretaceous Period, some 60 million years ago, most ancestors of modern sharks had appeared.

One of the early sharks evolved into mammoth proportions. *Carcharodon megalodon*, as it was called, appeared 50 million years ago and flourished for 35 million years. It resembled a great white shark except that it probably reached 40-some feet in length—twice the size of the great white. Its teeth were 6 inches long, and it had a mouth to match. Fossil teeth from this shark are still brought up by vessels dredging for manganese nodules in the South Pacific, as well as from various fossil sites on land.

Only 25 million years ago the ancestor of the hammerhead shark emerged. Its unusual head shape was thought to be a selective adaptation. The longevity of this type of shark, even though it is the youngest of all, indicates that it may be an evolutionary success rather than an experiment.

THE GLIDERS

The contention that sharks are inferior to other fish because they have cartilage instead of bone is unfounded. Cartilage is virtually weightless underwater, so a shark does not need a gas bladder to compensate for the weight of its skeleton as other fish do.

Without a gas bladder, a bony fish would crash to the bottom. With it, such a creature is a prisoner within a certain depth range. The pressure in the gas bladder must be slowly adjusted to ascend or descend beyond this range. Not so for the shark, master of the vertical. A shark can plummet to the depths or swim to the surface with relative impunity.

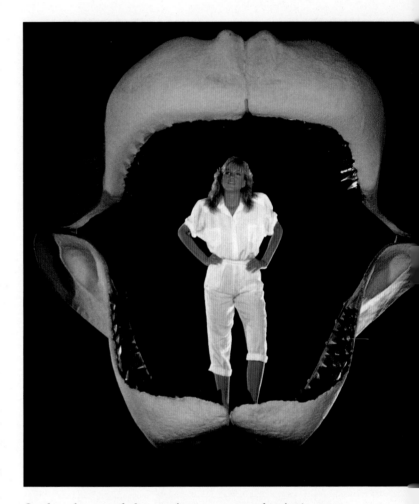

Carcharodon megalodon, a giant ancestor of today's great white shark, had jaws large enough to swallow a person whole. This reconstruction of a megalodon jaw at the Smithsonian Institute in Washington D.C. shows just how much of a bite this ancient shark had. Its huge teeth, like the great white's, were serrated like steak knives. It could cut through skin, muscle and bone with the ease of a laser.

This blacktip reef shark would sink if it stopped swimming for any length of time. But its broad pectoral fins, jutting out from its sides like the wings of an airplane, allow it to glide effortlessly. This shark can take a few strokes, then coast along, supported by its fins. A buoyant oil in its liver helps reduce the shark's weight underwater. Bottom-dwelling sharks are able to pump water over their gills to breathe.

Nurse sharks spend much of their time resting in caves and crevices, often in small groups. They usually prey on small invertebrates, but they can muster up enough enthusiasm to gobble a fish. Though placid by nature, when provoked they can snap at divers. Some open-water sharks also rest in caves, appearing to be asleep. Evidently such creatures do not have to continuously move to ensure a flow of water over their gills for respiration.

Many people believe sharks must always be swimming or they will drown for lack of a flow of oxygen-rich water over their gills. However, bottom-dwelling species like angel, horn, and swell sharks lie on the sea floor for hours, if not days, without any problems.

Although large, fast-moving sharks do seem to swim almost constantly, some have been seen resting in caves off the Yucatan Peninsula and Japan. Scientists believe these caves may provide an upwelling of fresh water so rich in oxygen that the sharks don't need to move. Moreover, the motion of fresh water may drive away parasites crawling around on the sharks' hides.

When a shark is swimming, relatively little energy is expended. Its triangular body, flattened along the belly and thin on top, is very streamlined. Its long, broad pectoral fins provide lift, much like the wings of a glider. Thus, a shark is able to swim a few leisurely strokes, then glide along like a bird. Its modest underwater weight is balanced to a considerable extent by its liver, which is loaded with buoyant oil.

SHINING WHITE TEETH

Oddly enough, a shark has no teeth—at least as we know them. Its "teeth" are really modified scales, but they still work very well. Each species' teeth are particularly well suited for biting into their favorite prey.

Bottom-dwelling sharks often have sharp, inward-pointing teeth for seizing and holding prey. Larger, fish-eating sharks generally have long, daggerlike teeth for tearing into the fishes' vitals and breaking them into bite-sized chunks. Some sharks have needlelike spikes at the bottom of each fang, perhaps for holding prey. The tiger shark's teeth are probably designed for slicing through flesh and bone as well as for grasping.

Several species have teeth that are serrated like steak knives. The great white, the bull, and the dusky have triangular, serrated upper teeth for shearing through muscle and bone, while the lower teeth are more pointed, perhaps for holding as well as for cutting. The whale shark, the largest of all, has thousands of teeth, but

The oceanic whitetip shark glides effortlessly on its broad, winglike pectoral fins. The striped fish accompanying this formidable predator are pilotfish. Supposedly, pilotfish guide sharks to prey. In reality, the pilotfish enjoy a meal ticket from the scraps left by the shark. In return, the pilotfish will clean the shark of parasites on its hide. Pilotfish can grow up to about 18 inches long.

A mako shark is gingerly examined. Armed with stilleto-sharp, inward-facing teeth, the mako shark's jaw is designed for catching and holding prey. Although mako is the name given to this shark in many parts of the world, the same shark is also called the bonito shark off California.

This sight has sent shivers down many a person's spine. Nothing matches the view of a great white shark rearing its head out of the water, jaws agape. In some parts of the world, great whites deliberately poke their snouts out of the water to spot seals hauled out on rocks. Sometimes these sharks will even lunge out of the water at prey.

they are a modest eighth of an inch or so long, sufficient because the whale shark feeds mainly on tiny planktonic forms.

Because shark teeth are actually a type of scale, they can be easily replaced. Most sharks have several rows of teeth. While at least one row is in use, the others lie like fallen dominoes, ready to move into place when one is lost. The teeth are not rooted deeply into the jaw; instead they are attached to the gums.

Shark scales are called denticles, and with good reason—they are like sharp, pointed teeth. Each one is usually slanted toward the tail for streamlining. Because of this, the hide feels smooth one way and very abrasive the other. In fact, shark skin is so rough that the coastal Indians once used it as sandpaper. Even today, a few discerning wood sculptors favor shark skin over sandpaper.

HOUND OF THE SEA

With remarkable perception the ancient Greeks dubbed the shark "hound of the sea." Today we know that some sharks are capable of detecting a single part of blood diluted in as much as 100 million parts of seawater. Roughly two-thirds of a shark's brain is geared toward receiving and interpreting olfactory signals.

The shark has been called the "living nose," and with considerable justification. When a shark picks up a scent from a wounded creature, it begins tracking it. The shark swims in a zigzag fashion, swinging its head from side to side to determine the direction the odor is coming from.

Although a shark may not always be in a position to smell its prey, it can still hear it from a considerable distance. The shark is very sensitive to low-frequency sounds. It can easily hear a struggling fish or some other creature thrashing about on the surface.

Other senses come into play as the shark nears its prey. Disturbances in the water can be picked up by the lateral line, a row of pores lined with sensitive nerve endings on either side of the shark. The shark probably *feels* rather than hears with its lateral line, in somewhat the same way as we feel a breeze on our cheeks.

Even if a shark's prey stops moving and makes no sound, it can still be detected. Tiny flasklike pores on the shark's head, called *ampullae of Lorenzini*, are lined with nerve endings. These pick up electrical impulses generated by muscular action. Any living creature can thus

The hammerhead shark's strange snout has provoked many interesting theories. Some say it acts like an airplane wing, allowing the shark to skim along just over the sand, searching for prey. Others claim it separates the shark's sensory organs, giving it a superior sense of direction and a broader searching range when hunting down prey. One diver saw a hammerhead use one side of its head to pin a stingray to the sea floor so the shark could swivel around and bite the ray in front, immobilizing it.

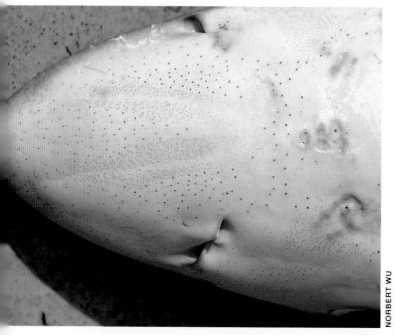

NORBERT WU

The pores of this shark's head (above) are called *ampullae of Lorenzini,* or "flasks" of Lorenzini. These vial-shaped openings, filled with mucus, sense electrical impulses given off by living organisms. In test conditions, sharks have been able to consistently locate prey sealed in special chambers that block out visual, chemical, and even physical—the sense of touch—stimuli. The ampullae of Lorenzini are probably very important to the deep sea cat shark (right), which also has quite large eyes. Like those of a cat, these eyes are lined with mirrorlike plates that reflect "lost" light back into the retina so the shark can see in near darkness.

be located by the shark. The ampullae are also sensitive to changes in the temperature, chemistry, and physical properties of the water.

Vision is generally not important in initially locating prey. Along many parts of the West Coast, clarity underwater often extends only a few feet—sometimes far less. Off Hawaii, the visibility can be much better—sometimes over 100 feet—but even so, sight is useful only as the shark closes in for the kill.

A shark's vision is still probably quite good, for its eyes are filled with rods that enable it to see objects in dim light against contrasting backgrounds. Moreover, mirrorlike silvery plates, called *tapetum lucidum*, bounce "lost" light back into the retina. When the light is bright, black pigment cells—unique to sharks—slide over these plates and the pupils contract. (Bony fish cannot adjust their pupils; another indication of the shark's superiority.)

The shark may not be able to discern colors well, if at all, but everything except green and blue is filtered out beyond 120 feet of depth anyway. A shark cannot perceive much detail either, but its other senses guide it straight to its prey. Finally, many sharks have a tough, protective membrane called a *nictitans* that covers their eyes as they bite, so they don't actually see their prey as they attack.

Sharks may taste their prey, though, for they do not swallow everything they bite. If a morsel doesn't seem right, they spit it out. Whether this is determined by feel or by taste, no one knows.

The tiger shark seems to be among the least discriminating feeders, for stomach examinations have revealed bizarre items from native tom-tom drums to coils of copper wire, and from conch shells to human limbs. Several grisly remains have turned up off of Hawaii.

SUGGESTED READING

COUSTEAU, JACQUES YVES, and PHILIPPE COUSTEAU. *The Shark: Splendid Savage of the Sea.* Garden City, New York: Doubleday and Company, 1970.

ELLIS, RICHARD. *The Book of Sharks.* New York: Grosset and Dunlap, 1975.

LINEAWEAVER, THOMAS H. and RICHARD H. BACKUS. *The Natural History of Sharks.* Garden City, New York: Doubleday and Company, 1973.

MOSS, SANFORD A. *Sharks: An Introduction for the Amateur Naturalist.* Edgewood Cliffs, New Jersey: Prentice-Hall, Inc., 1984.

Large sharks, like this blue (above) protect their eyes when attacking prey. Although they have upper and lower eyelids, the lids are scarcely movable. But a third eyelid, the nictitans, slides into place by reflex whenever anything is close to the eyes. The nictitans is opaque and blocks out all vision for a moment. Some sharks simply roll their eyeballs back when they attack, protecting the cornea by hiding it. As this blue shark (below) attacks a shark cage, it protects its eyes. The shark was lured to the cage with bleeding fish.

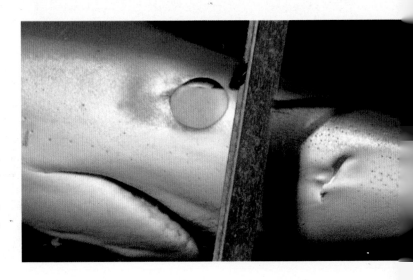

The tiger shark will eat just about anything. Incredible assortments of items, many inedible, have been found in tiger sharks' stomachs. Everything from boat cushions to tin cans and from wallets to nuts and bolts have been discovered in their stomachs. Once an unopened can of salmon was found—too bad the shark couldn't open it.

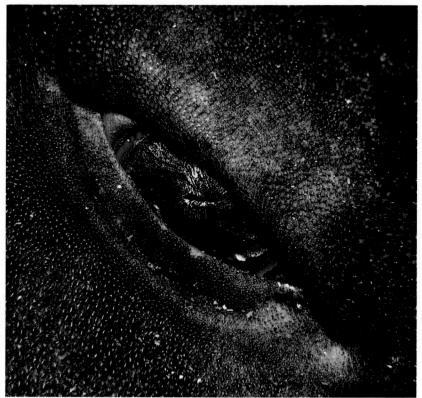

The swell shark's eye is a good example of the variety of texture, form, and color found in shark eyes. Some sharks have round pupils, some, goatlike slits. Others have series of tiny points. Most are designed to adjust to a wide range of light, particularly since many sharks are nocturnal feeders.

The Rogue's Gallery

Dozens of species of sharks frequent the West Coast. Many specialize in one type of food and are adapted for a particular habitat.

The horn shark's drab, mottled body enables it to hide under ledges so that it is very difficult to spot. A spine at the base of each dorsal fin discourages other fish from making a meal of the horn shark. But the shark itself has several rows of sharp teeth admirably suited for tearing into prey. Behind these teeth are others that resemble a cobblestone pavement; these are designed for crushing mollusks.

The grasp of the horn shark's teeth can be very gentle. When eggs, which are encapsulated in tough, leathery pouches, are laid, the female carefully picks them up in her mouth and places them in protected crevices in the rocks.

The swell shark, or puffer shark as it is sometimes called, shares the horn shark's habitat. When the swell shark is threatened, it quickly swallows water, inflating itself to several times its normal girth. If it is hauled out of the water, it will readily swallow air instead. Sometimes it will even clamp its teeth onto its tail so a predator cannot devour it. As if this were not enough, the flesh is rather noxious—in fact, its meat is downright poisonous to humans.

The horn shark lays its eggs in a tough case that feels like plastic. Although the horn shark's teeth are needle-sharp, the mother shark is so gentle that she can carry her eggs to protected crevices in the rocks without piercing them.

MARTY SNYDERMAN

The horn shark is a small creature that seldom grows much over a yard long. It feeds on mollusks, crustaceans, and small fish. Heavy spines at the base of its dorsal fins discourage larger predators from swallowing it. The horn shark frequents rocky ledges and crevices.

The swell shark is a sluggish animal that inhabits rocky reefs. It defends itself by swallowing water, inflating its belly to the size of a basketball. As if this were not enough, its flesh is toxic.

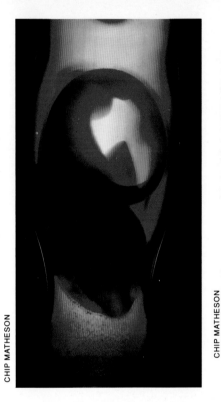

CHIP MATHESON

CHIP MATHESON

Some sharks are born live. Others hatch from eggs inside the mother, then emerge alive. Still others, like this swell shark (left) hatch from eggs made from tough, leathery pouches. The tiny shark (above) comes complete with teeth however, and ready for action.

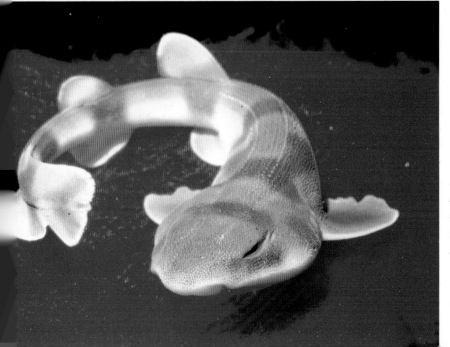

Infant sharks are called pups. This swell shark pup probably wouldn't fit everyone's concept of an ideal pet, although it does have some appeal in its own right. This little shark could grow to three feet or so.

17

The angel shark relies more on cunning than on chemical warfare. It buries itself in the sand by fluttering its flattened pectoral fins. Once covered, it is virtually invisible to prey and predator alike.

THE HUNTER'S SECRETS

The hammerhead shark, found off southern California and Hawaii, is an expert at ferreting out stingrays completely buried in the sand. What its strange snout can't sniff or see, it can sense; its head is a marvel of sophisticated detection gear.

The hammerhead may be more sensitive to electrical impulses than any other creature on earth. Its broad head is liberally endowed with ampullae of Lorenzini, which pick up the electrical impulses generated by the muscular actions of other living creatures (see preceding chapter). The wide-set eyes and nostrils also probably give it a keen directional sense so it can home in on its prey. Its odd snout may even have a hydrodynamic advantage, allowing it to plane along just off the ocean floor, ready to vacuum up its hapless prey.

This angel shark is no angel. With its mottled hide, it can lie camouflaged in the sand, waiting for an unwary victim to swim by. Unlike many larger sharks, the angel shark can remain virtually motionless for hours, if not days. Oxygen-rich water flows over its gills through vents called spiracles. The gridlike patterns in each opening are the gill rakers of this shark. The angel shark is flat, enabling it to lie on patches of sand without being easily seen. Even its eyes blend in with the bottom.

Several species of hammerhead sharks inhabit the Pacific. Th scalloped hammerheads get their name from the wavy lea edge of their strange head. By contrast, the smooth hammerh shows a nearly perfect crescent along the front of its head. bonnethead has a narrower head which makes it look as if it v wearing a bonnet. Hammerheads form large schools in California, Mexico. Fortunately, they are usually not particu aggressive toward divers, although they can be dangerous. largest hammerheads can stretch over 20 feet in le

Why do some sharks leap out of the water? Do they hope to knock off parasites as they splash down? Are they showing off or making a territorial display to other sharks? Are they escaping larger predators or scaring prey into tight groups? Or do they just like to jump? No one knows for sure, although threshers, which are fine game fish, will perform high jumps when hooked. Threshers are good-eating fish. In the past, they were often sold as swordfish by unscrupulous restauranteurs. Today, many people prefer shark over swordfish.

Many ideas have been advanced to explain the common thresher shark's tail, which often equals the length of its body. Some say the thresher uses its tail like a whip, lashing or cutting its prey to stun it. Others claim it herds small fish into a tight circle with its tail, then picks them off. A few even maintain that it swats its prey out of the water with its tail. We do know one thing for certain—the common thresher can swim fast enough with its tail to leap completely out of the water. No one knows why it does this.

The bigeye thresher inhabits deeper regions of the Pacific. Its huge eyes, often larger than coffee mugs, probably help it to detect prey in the darkness of the depths.

Cat sharks also seem to see well in the dark. But when they are exposed to the light, their pupils contract nearly horizontally into a series of tiny points quite unlike any feline. Three species of cat sharks are found along the West Coast, all in deep water.

TOM MYERS

This cat shark seems to be sniffing the sea floor. Cat sharks are quite diversified. They inhabit shallow and deep waters throughout the Pacific. One species is found only in the Gulf of California. Some species are quite rare, with only a few individuals known to science.

South Pacific

Some sharks range throughout the tropic to subtemperate waters of the Pacific. The blue shark, the oceanic whitetip, even the Galapagos shark pictured here, enjoy a widespread distribution. They seem to travel wherever the current—and their prey—take them. Some are just as likely to show up off Baja California as they are off Hawaii. Some, like the cat shark and hammerhead, are represented by many species, while others are unique.

ED ROBINSON

Contrary to its name the Galapagos shark is found worldwide in warm and temperate waters. It seems to prefer islands, and it may be found everywhere from the Galapagos Islands to Hawaii. It is also found off Central and South America. The Galapagos shark can be quite aggressive.

NORBERT WU

This colorful little devil, called a zebra horn shark, is typical of smaller fish of the tropical Pacific. Its bright colors and irregular patterns allow it to blend into its surroundings, which are often every bit as colorful.

The Throwbacks

Although the horn shark, mentioned earlier, is among the most ancient forms, sixgill, sevengill, and frilled sharks all have ancient relatives. These three are readily distinguished by their single dorsal fin and six or more gill slits. All other West Coast sharks have only five.

Sixgill and sevengill sharks seem to prefer silty bays, although they do range into deep water. The sixgill has also been called the comb-toothed shark because each lower cusp has several comblike ridges, while the uppers are more ordinary in appearance.

Nothing is ordinary about the frilled shark. Its first gill slit extends underneath the neck to each side, unlike any other shark. The five other slits, also laced with frills, fall into the usual position. The frilled shark, like its ancient relatives and its rare cousin, the well-named megamouth shark, has a mouth that ends almost at the tip of its snout.

DANIEL W. GOTSHALL

This young sevengill shark is a throwback to ancient sharks that lived hundreds of millions of years ago. While most "modern" sharks have five gills, this shark has seven. This animal frequents bays from Chile to British Columbia, although it is not found in the tropics.

The sixgill shark can be a real bruiser, growing as long as perhaps 15 feet and weighing several hundred pounds. Though common, it is seldom seen by divers, which is just as well since it can be quite aggressive. Like the sevengill, it is a throwback to earlier times. This specimen was swimming off Vancouver Island, British Columbia, Canada.

THOMAS E. HAIGHT

The megamouth shark, so named because of its cavernous mouth, is among the rarest of West Coast sharks. Fortunately for the diver (above), the megamouth is a gentle creature that feeds on tiny planktonic organisms. Like its relatives, the basking shark and the whale shark, the megamouth sports rows of tiny teeth and gill rakers that are modified into brushlike filters for feeding. Unlike its kin, however, the megamouth generally stays in deep water. This particular specimen was captured live in a fisherman's net and brought to the harbor at Dana Point, California. It was studied by scientists for a day—the only recorded examination of a living megamouth—then released. A radiotag attached to its hide indicated that the shark swam very slowly—only half a mile an hour or so.

Blue Water

Some sharks thrive in open water, preying on fast-moving schooling fish and squid. The ubiquitous blue shark is among the most successful inhabitants of this realm, and a close examination will reveal why.

From its sharply pointed nose to its graceful tail, the slender blue is sleek and hydrodynamic. Its scythe-shaped pectorals seem particularly well suited for gliding through the water. Even its color pattern is efficient; iridescent dark blue on top so it can easily blend in with the depths when seen from above, and white underneath, making it difficult to spot from below.

At first glance the bonito shark, or *mako* as it is called in other areas, resembles a large, heavy blue shark. But despite its stockier appearance, nothing is sluggish about its movements.

Like members of the tuna family, the bonito shark has a stiff, symmetrical tail. Also like the tuna, it is warm-blooded. Its body is 18° F warmer than the surrounding water, which triples its muscular efficiency. Its tissues are heated when venous blood, warmed by metabolic processes, passes through a parallel network of vessels and warms the cooler arterial blood. This hot blood rushes through muscles as tough as those of an ox in a body more streamlined than a torpedo. Consequently, the bonito shark can chase down the fastest prey.

The oceanic whitetip shark, a slower, offshore species, occasionally turns up along the southern California coast. Like other warm water creatures, it may be more prevalent when El Niño, a southern current, brings balmy water to our coast. This happens every several years.

Shark billies are nothing more than sticks or poles used by divers to fend off sharks. Sometimes a nail protrudes through the business end for encouraging sharks to leave. The trick is to discourage the shark, not to anger it. The shark billy is widely used by safety divers while filming is underway.

This blue shark has seized a mackerel, among its favorite food. Sharks that hunt in open water are generally large—so they won't become prey—and fast. Anything that survives in open water, without shelter, must be swift and agile, and the blue shark is certainly that.

MARTY SNYDERMAN

Not all sharks caught by fishermen are brought to market. Blue sharks are not widely accepted as a food fish because of their disagreeable ammonia taste. Consequently, they are usually tossed overboard, dead or sometimes wounded. This blue shark had been tangled in a plastic monofilament net which severely cut its mouth. Doomed to die from its injuries, this shark joins literally millions of animals condemned as "trash fish." Marine mammals have also perished in huge numbers in certain types of nets.

DEAN DE PHILLIPO

This whitetip reef shark inhabits tropical waters throughout much of the Pacific. It is very territorial and seldom strays from its home. During the day, it often rests in caves. It usually feeds at night.

This bonito shark, or mako, is a close relative of the great white. It is an extremely swift, agile predator found in most tropical to subtemperate seas throughout the world. The streamers on this shark's dorsal are from a parasite.

NORBERT WU

The tiger shark is a fearless, unpredictable creature. It does attack humans on occasion. Generally found in tropical waters throughout the Pacific, it sometimes appears as far north as southern California, where it is not particularly welcomed by divers. Fortunately, only one person is believed to have been attacked by a tiger shark in California, although off Hawaii and other parts of the Pacific, attacks are more common. The tiger shark grows to a least 18 feet in length.

Unwelcome Guests

A number of species of reef sharks are found in Hawaii. Though relatively small, they can be dangerous, especially to people spearing fish.

The tiger shark—not to be confused with the diminutive leopard shark—is found in Hawaiian waters, and also visits our coast when the water is warm. Unlike the oceanic whitetip shark, however, it will venture quite close to shore where it is most unwelcome because it is quite dangerous.

The tiger is distinguished by its broad, blunt snout which is almost squared off at the end. The pups—as the grinning youngsters of all sharks are called—have splotches on their backs reminiscent of the markings of tigers.

The pups of many large predatory species, including the tiger sharks, hatch out in the oviduct, feed on the yolk of their egg, and never form any connection to the mother. Conversely, other species, including the blue and the hammerhead, do form an umbilicus of sorts. Both methods produce live young—tiny versions of the adults ready to swim and search for food.

Even less welcome than the tiger shark is the bull shark, which once went by many aliases; but it is now recognized as one species wherever it goes. Because it can tolerate fresh water, it was variously called the Lake Zambezi shark, the Lake Nicaragua shark, and the Ganges shark. It thrives in the Tigris and Euphrates rivers of the Middle East, in the Amazon River, and even in some streams in the southeastern United States. It also inhabits most temperate seas of the world, including the waters of southern Australia, where it is known as the whaler. In nearly all these places, the bull shark has become notorious for its attacks on humans. Fortunately, it is rare off the West Coast of the United States.

The bull shark is among the most vicious of sharks. It has a nasty habit of swimming up rivers and staying in lakes. Lake Nicaragua, Lake Zambezi, the Tigris, the Euphrates, the Ganges River—to name a few—are all infested with bull sharks. This animal also frequents coastal waters.

The leopard shark, despite its ferocious name, is harmless. A small shark, it seldom grows to more than about four or five feet in length. It is commonly seen by divers from Mexico to Oregon. The leopard shark frequents shallow reefs and sand flats. The red, plantlike structure next to this baby leopard is a colonial animal called a gorgonian, or sea fan.

The great white shark is the fiercest fish on earth. It can grow to nearly 20 feet in length—if not more—and weighs tons. It can dice 300-pound seals up into a few bite-sized chunks, or chomp a person in half. The great white is a top-level predator, surpassed only by humans. Yet despite its reputation, very few people have been attacked, considering the number of people in the water at any one time. In reality, we humans have done far more harm to the magnificent creature than it has to us. In many parts of the world, great whites are becoming scarce. Tooth-lined jaws are prized as trophies, even though the shark itself is often thrown overboard. Fortunately, a number of people throughout the world are recognizing the great white as a creature worth preserving; in some areas, people even lobby to have the great white declared an endangered species so it can be protected. Certainly the great white remains one of the all-time biggest challenges for underwater photographers.

swims quite smoothly, often with the relentless momentum of a freight train. The concentration of bulky muscle along its streamlined body gives it tremendous power and speed. The great white is also warm-blooded, an attribute which makes its muscles much stronger.

A few great whites have been observed feeding, usually on a piece of bait dangled from the side of a boat. When the shark seems sure of its prey, it will approach steadily, with no hesitation or preliminary passes, and take its first bite. If the prey is to its liking, and it wants more, the great white will return, sometimes not until several minutes have passed. Although virtually nothing can stop it, the shark's movements are so graceful as to seem almost leisurely even when it is actually moving rather swiftly.

The great white shark's bite is awesome—its serrated teeth are as sharp as scalpels. A 14-foot specimen caught off Santa Catalina Island had the remains of two harbor seals in its stomach, each neatly diced into several chunks. The shark's teeth had severed head, bone, and muscle as surely as a cleaver. One of the seals weighed 175 pounds—the other 125.

Most sharks do bite with considerable force. A dusky shark's jaw pressure was once measured at nearly 20 tons per square inch, and the dusky is a much smaller shark than the great white.

The great white is a top-level predator. Elephant seals and harbor seals seem to be its favorite prey, while sea lions, sea otters, and probably fur seals are also devoured from time to time. For this reason, great whites lurk near seal and sea lion rookeries (breeding grounds), although some also prowl about offshore, feeding on a variety of fish.

Some authorities and fishermen feel that great whites may be more prevalent today than they were in the past few decades. Marine mammal populations have increased dramatically as a result of various conservation measures. Great whites, major predators of such populations, may have increased their numbers as a result.

Other people, particularly some of the commercial fishermen in southern California, think the great whites have always been around but that few people were interested in them until recently. No market existed for great whites then, while today they are becoming increasingly popular in fish markets. Also, their jaws and teeth are now of considerable value as souvenirs.

THE FIERCEST FISH

The great white is not a common shark, either in numbers or when compared to other sharks. Once seen, however, it is not easily forgotten. It is a husky shark, with an impressive girth—one 17-footer had a circumference of 13 feet!

The great white carries its weight well. It

31

Like a great whale, a 30-foot basking shark leaps out of the water, to fall back with a huge splash. No one knows why they do this. Such a sight is rare; many people have observed basking sharks for years and never seen one jump. The author only succeeded in getting this photograph after 20-some years of effort.

This salmon shark's gums are the same color as the flesh of its favorite prey. The salmon shark is a close relative of the great white shark.

The salmon shark, occasionally called the Pacific porbeagle, is well known to many fishermen in northern California, Oregon, and Washington. It is closely related to the great white, although it specializes in fish, including salmon. Its teeth reflect this specialization—they are daggerlike, with small spines at the base of each blade for holding prey.

Salmon sharks sometimes gather at the mouths of streams, particularly in the Pacific Northwest, as steelhead and salmon begin their spawning runs. Consequently, salmon sharks are not popular with fishermen.

THE GENTLE GIANTS

The largest fish, like the largest whales (which are mammals), are among the most gentle creatures on earth. The basking shark, which probably reaches more than 40 feet in length, seems intent mainly upon going about its business of straining tiny planktonic organisms from the sea. Its mammoth gill rakers, which filter out the plankton, are equal to the task—a 20-some-footer can force about 4 million pounds of seawater through its maw every hour.

Like teeth, the gill rakers are replaced periodically; but unlike teeth, they must grow in. This means the basking shark may have to go hungry for a while. A British scientist believes the basking shark may hibernate, in a sense, slowing its metabolism and living off the fat in its liver until its gill rakers grow back. Other authorities theorize that the gill rakers are replaced quickly so the basking shark does not have to fast for long periods.

Once the basking shark begins to feed again, it cruises placidly along at about two knots (approximately 2.5 miles per hour), a speed that can be easily equaled by a good swimmer. Its cavernous white mouth yawns open to the sea like the cowling of a jet engine.

But this leviathan is not always tranquil. Occasionally, the basking shark can be seen playing tag or follow-the-leader with its mates. Sometimes it chases other sharks around in a tight circle, or leaps completely out of the water like a breaching whale. No one knows why it performs these antics, which always seems to be a good reason for armchair philosophers to come up with any number of ingenious explanations.

Big enough to swallow a horse, this basking shark instead is swallowing tiny organisms floating in the water. The basking shark's gill rakers are modified into brushlike combs which strain small animals from the sea. Basking sharks, whale sharks, and the strange megamouth are all plankton feeders, like the great whales. And like whales, they are generally peaceful creatures, tolerating the presence of humans with benign indifference. They will often allow divers to hitch a ride by hanging onto their fins, although a quick flip of their heavy tail could easily crush a person.

The whale shark is the largest fish in the sea. It reaches over 40 feet in length, and possibly as much as 60. Fortunately for these two divers, the whale shark is a gentle animal that doesn't seem bothered by their presence. The huge shark tolerates other hitchhikers as well: remoras cluster near its mouth. The remora (right) often clings to sharks for a free meal. In return, the remora will pick parasites from the shark's hide.

This activity is also true of the whale shark—the world's largest fish. It has been observed swimming toward boats with its huge mouth agape, or bobbing up and down among schools of tuna. Although it has a small gullet, it may gobble down a few fish in the process. Fish do try to swim away from danger, so they might even unintentionally help the shark by frantically flailing their way down the huge funnel of its mouth.

Certainly the whale shark consumes smaller fish. Anchovies, sardines, other schooling fish, and squid are inhaled in droves. But the whale shark also strains plankton from the sea, making it a cosmopolitan feeder like some of the great whales.

Unlike many of the whales that migrate to polar feeding grounds in the summer, the whale shark remains in warm water year-round, seldom venturing farther north than La Jolla, California.

The whale shark is rare, or perhaps it simply spends most of its time submerged; consequently we know very little about it. It very likely exceeds 40 feet in length, and could possibly reach 60-some feet, although no specimen that size has ever been accurately measured.

One of the whale shark's secrets has been revealed, however. In 1953, a trawler brought up a large shark egg case from the Gulf of Mexico. Inside the case was an almost fully developed embryo of a whale shark, 14.5 inches long—a humble beginning for the world's largest fish!

SUGGESTED READING

Budker, Paul. *The Life of Sharks*. New York: Columbia University Press, 1971.

Miller, Daniel J. and Robert N. Lea. *Guide to the Coastal Marine Fishes of California*. Sacramento: State of California Department of Fish and Game, 1972.

Sibley, Gretchen ed. *Biology of the White Shark*. Los Angeles: Southern California Academy of Sciences, 1985.

The whale shark never seems common, but once seen, it is never forgotten. Although this shark would appear to have no need for camouflage, it does sport numerous spots, and rows of spots, on its back. Unlike other sharks, it has several longitudinal ridges along its back. Combined with the rows of spots, the whale shark's back can seem like a giant checkerboard.

The Hunters and the Hunted

Even the patient basking shark can get riled. When kayake
Larry Kepko approached this shark too swiftly, the huge anima
spooked, shearing off to one side to avoid the kayak
The upper lobe of the shark's tail (above) inadvertently slappe
Kepko on his back, leaving an indelible imprint on his shi
(right). Despite the size and generally sluggish nature of thes
animals, they can move very fast when agitated. Thi
photograph was taken at 1/250th of a second
yet it did not freeze the motion of the shark's tai

The shark has been respected longer than it has been reviled, for it is more benefactor than malefactor. To many ancient cultures the shark meant food, tools, and weapons. To some early people the shark was a god to be venerated. Even the European explorers did not loathe nor fear the shark—to them it was just another fish in a strange new world.

It was not long before the shark was noticed, and from there it was but a short step to exploitation. The slow-moving, peaceful basking shark was an easy target. Whalers found they could augment their precious casks of whale oil with another valuable commodity. The basking shark's liver was rich with an oil that was every bit as good for lamps as the best sperm whale oil.

But the whaling industry faltered after the dawn of the petroleum age, and for a while the basking shark was left in peace. During World War II, however, the basking shark was again harvested for its liver, as was the soupfin shark—this time as a source of vitamin A, which was given to bomber pilots to improve their night vision. Fortunately for both species, a synthetic substitute was formulated in 1947, although soupfins continue to be harvested to some extent.

Other species were not so lucky. The bonito shark, with its habit of leaping spectacularly out of the water, attracted anglers. Charles Frederick Holder, founder of the elite Tuna Club of Catalina Island, called the bonito shark "a trim cavalier." As early as 1910 he described bonito sharks and others following a tuna school:

> Hanging on the outer edge of the great school, and lurking beneath it, was a band of desperate hulking villains. . . lurching along like wolves preying upon sheep.

With descriptions like this in vogue, it became a civic duty to rid the world of such terrible creatures, to say nothing of its being a great sport.

The sight of a tall, triangular dorsal fin slicing the water has sent many a swimmer or scuba diver racing for shore. In this case, however, the fin belongs to a basking shark placidly feeding near the coast of Santa Barbara, California, a reminder that big sharks can travel wherever they please.

Kayaker John Erickson enjoys paddling with enormous basking sharks. His kayak is less than 18 feet long, and the sharks are often nearly twice that length. The sharks are friendly, even curious, when approached gently.

The Pacific angel shark, unlike the stereotype shark, spends much of its time buried in the sand, where its mottled form is difficult to see. When disturbed, it erupts from the bottom in a cloud of sand. Sometimes, especially at night, the angel shark grows active and begins to prowl over its domain. Its mouth is lined with needlelike teeth designed for catching and holding small fish and squid which are common in its domain. Sometimes the predator becomes prey, however. Larger sharks and even black sea bass are known to devour angel sharks.

Today the bonito shark remains a prime game fish, often the top catch in shark fishing derbies. It is also very good eating, unlike some other sharks—particularly blues—which are sometimes caught in droves, killed, photographed, and discarded.

Sharks were once considered "trash fish" in commercial fisheries too, not because they were actually bad to eat, but because no market existed for them. After all, who would want to eat a shark?

Simple economics dispelled the public's reservations about sharks as food. Soon, many species that were caught incidentally with other fish were saved instead of being tossed back into the sea. A few, like the thresher, became so popular that important commercial fisheries developed around them. In time, a market was created for leopard and angel sharks. Even the great white, actually fine for eating, was utilized. "Eat the shark before it eats you," became the motto.

SHARK ATTACKS

Sharks are far tastier to us than we are to them. Although dozens of people have been sampled by sharks along the West Coast, nearly all of them have been rejected.

Robert Pamperin wasn't.

Pamperin was skin diving off La Jolla, California, in 1959 when, according to his companion, a huge shark swallowed him up to his waist. No trace of him was found, even though a thorough search was made the same day.

Some felt that the incident was an elaborate insurance hoax—others believed he had been attacked by a great white shark. But Pamperin's buddy claimed that the shark, which was nearly 20-feet long, had a blunt nose, a slender body, and a long upper tail lobe—all of which suggested a tiger shark. Also, the water had been warmer than usual, and tiger sharks had been known to eat humans in other parts of the world, including Hawaii. At any rate, Robert Pamperin is the only diver believed to have been killed and eaten by a shark in southern California. The remains of a few people have turned up in the stomachs of tiger sharks in Hawaii, although such attacks are quite rare.

Leopard sharks are small, fish-eating sharks common in shallow water. Generally, they can be approached quite closely if a diver moves slowly.

This little horn shark is quite at home among the rocky reefs of the West Coast. Surrounded by purple sea urchins, this horn shark has an assured supply of food. It has special crushing teeth designed for cracking shells, but it also has sharp cutting teeth so it can seize fish.

Hammerheads are fish-eating sharks whose teeth are designed for seizing, then slicing prey. Despite their odd-shaped head, which some have said is clumsy, they are agile, aggressive predators and can be dangerous to humans.

Sharks are easily lured within camera range by chumming with bait fish. Divers must be very careful, however. Sharks like this blue, or like oceanic whitetip or reef whitetip sharks, can go into a feeding frenzy when food is present, sometimes even biting each other.

A spear fisherman was bitten by a small hammerhead off La Jolla. The small hammerhead is a species also associated with warm water. Later, off Malibu, another spear fisherman swam up to a school of blue sharks in the midst of a feeding frenzy, and was bitten for his trouble. The only other person attacked by a blue shark was a Navy diver off Coronado in 1952. Despite their bad reputation and great numbers, blue sharks rarely attack people.

Only five other known attacks have occurred in southern California. Three were made by small, unidentified sharks in shallow water; one involved a great white shark that bit a diver on his thigh at San Miguel Island. The man had been diving for abalones near a major seal rookery when he was attacked. The most recent incident involved a woman in a sea kayak who was killed by a great white. Her companion was never found.

In spite of these incidents, considering the tremendous popularity of water sports in southern California and Hawaii, statistics prove that both areas have been remarkably safe over the years.

This hammerhead shark at Sea Life Park in Hawaii is a star attraction. Large predators have always fascinated people, and sharks are no exception. But even as people marvel at the power of these animals, they also admire their grace. Once the public gets to know such creatures, they understand them better. The ultimate value in having animals in captivity is to educate the public, to foster in people understanding and compassion toward animals. Without such familiarity, creatures like lions and bears would still be fearsome beasts to be hunted down and killed rather than respected as important animals that play a vital role in nature.

ED ROBINSON

An extraordinarily light-colored blue shark prowls the surface. Blue sharks pose little threat to humans. Most attacks have involved spearfishing enthusiasts carrying bleeding fish, or photographers deliberately attracting sharks with cut-up fish. Blue sharks prefer small prey and rarely attack large animals.

*Perhaps no animal can equal the great white shark in
generating fear and awe in a human. Not only is the shark
enormous, it is also dauntless; if the great white wants to
approach you, it will. Virtually nothing will stop a
determined great white*

DANGER: SHARKS

North of Point Conception, the dividing line between southern and central California, the sea changes dramatically. The northwest wind buffets the coast almost continuously, and large ocean swells, virtually unhampered by any island of protecting land mass, pound the shore incessantly. The water is considerably colder here. Only the hardiest organisms survive in this harsh world.

Although some swimmers brave these brisk waters during the warmer months of late summer and early fall, their numbers are small compared to the great masses of people blanketing southern California beaches almost year-round. Although skin diving and surfing have become increasingly popular farther north, comparatively few people are involved. Yet, more people have been attacked by great white sharks in this region than anywhere else in the world. Strangely, most of them were bitten at locations that are not particularly popular, even by central and northern California standards.

Based on this fact, it would be logical to assume that safety exists in numbers, but this is not necessarily true. People have been attacked

near rather lonely parts of the coast, probably because this is where the greatest concentration of white sharks is found. The sharks frequent such places because seals, their favorite prey, generally shun areas popular to humans. Thus the only safety in numbers lies in the odds that only one person out of several will be bitten. And, if one person is attacked, his chances of survival are greatly enhanced if others are there to help him.

The odds didn't work for Dale Webster and Jack Greenlaw. They were diving near Año Nuevo Island, a seal rookery northwest of Santa Cruz, California, when a shark bit Webster's foot, then slashed Greenlaw's hand. A third diver escaped unscathed. Near the same area a few years later, another diver had his flipper seized by a large shark, probably a great white, although he was untouched.

Año Nuevo is not a safe place to dive. Great white sharks are often seen there by fishermen, who sometimes lose their catch to

The great white shark is found worldwide in warm to subtemperate seas. It can be found well offshore, in open water, or literally in the breakers. The great white favors seals in its diet, which often brings it close to shore.

the sharks. Even more discouraging, the elephant seals that frequent the area occasionally emerge from the water with huge bites taken out of their sides.

The Farallon Islands off San Francisco are also inhabited by seals and sharks. Several divers have been attacked there, so it is not a terribly popular spot any more.

Tomales Point, at the head of Bodega Bay, has become so notorious for shark attacks that a sign has been posted to warn divers and swimmers of the danger. Tomales Point, like the other two areas, is frequented by seals.

Several other divers have been chewed at various locations along the central and northern California coast, but the seal rookeries remain the most dangerous areas to dive.

Why were the divers bitten? They could have been mistaken for seals, but most of the attacks seemed more like preliminary tastings because no chunks were actually taken out of the victims. Perhaps the taste of the wetsuits discouraged the sharks. Then too, water visibility was generally quite clear, suggesting that the sharks had the opportunity to inspect the divers before attacking.

Some authorities feel that sharks are very territorial and will drive out any large, potential competitors from their realm, either by threatening them with a series of rapid passes or by actually biting them. This could be done to protect a feeding ground, or perhaps even a nursery area.

The females of some species are known to take over certain areas for bearing their pups. They fast during this period and are very aggressive toward intruders into their domain. This could possibly account for the white shark's behavior in some instances, if the white, like others, does actually set up a nursery area.

Several swimmers and surfers have been attacked by sharks in central and northern California and Oregon. The pattern of these attacks has been quite different from the attacks on divers, however. As early as 1952, a body surfer off Pacific Grove, near Monterey, had a huge chunk bitten out of his thigh. As rescuers towed him to shore, he was repeatedly attacked by the shark. He died of his wounds.

A swimmer was attacked at Baker Beach, south of San Francisco, and mauled so badly that he died also, despite the heroic efforts of his fiancée to save him. She literally pulled him away from the shark. Near Aptos, a girl was so badly bitten that her leg had to be amputated.

Several surfboards have been attacked. Some victims received minor wounds or even escaped as the shark chewed on their surf-

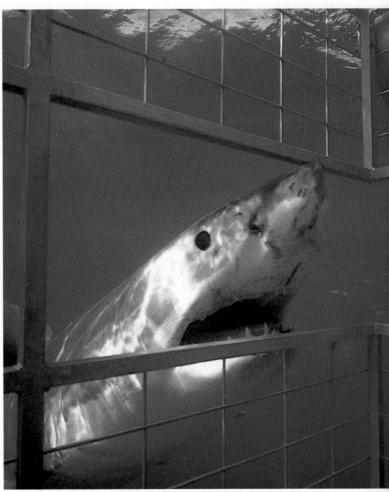

A shark cage must have a large enough opening to allow photographers plenty of clearance for filming. Too big a gap can be scary, however, as divers can discover. Sometimes a shark cage just isn't adequate.

boards. Others received major injuries and, in one instance, a shark bit through the surfboard as well as the surfer, killing him instantly.

These attacks on swimmers and surfers were generally quite aggressive, suggesting that the victims could have been mistaken for prey floundering about in the surf. Also, the turbid water near the surf line could have made it difficult for the shark to see what it was going to bite.

Even boats are not safe from the great white. A skiff towed behind a larger boat in Bodega Bay was reduced to matchwood by a large shark. A salmon trawler was attacked off the Klamath River by a great white, which left a tooth in the stern as a grim calling card.

SUGGESTED READING

BALDRIDGE, DAVID H. *Shark Attack.* New York: Berkley Publishing Corporation, 1974.

DAVIES, DAVID H. *About Sharks and Shark Attack.* New York: Hobbs, Dorman and Company, 1974.

This great white could sever the diver's hand in one bite, but fortunately, it is concentrating on the fish. Several products, ranging from horse meat to mackerel, are used to lure great whites into range for filming. Fortunately, more money can now be made filming these animals than killing them.

Overleaf: This grey reef shark is sharply silhouetted above the sea fan of a coral reef. Photo by Marty Snyderman.

MARTY SNYDERMAN

A few thousand dollars may seem like a lot of money for a diving suit, but for this diver, it is dirt cheap. This suit, made of stainless steel chain mail, protects divers against small sharks like this blue. Such suits are useful for filming or for other operations during which divers must work near aggressive sharks. They do not provide adequate protection from big sharks, however.

Sharks are undisputed champions of their oceanic realm. They boast a far lengthier heritage than most creatures on earth, proof of their success in a hostile environment.

Sharks and Our Future

Although dozens of people have been attacked by sharks on the West Coast and Hawaii, and particularly off central and northern California, only a few persons have been killed. Most of us nonchalantly face a greater hazard nearly every day—on the freeway.

We are generally far more dangerous to sharks than they are to us. Commercial fishermen worldwide catch millions of sharks every season to satisfy the growing demand for this fine source of food. And, more species are exploited as the popularity of shark meat increases.

Tragically, some people still view the shark much as our pioneers, in understandable ignorance, saw the wolf, the cougar, and the eagle—creatures now rarely observed.

The shark has earned its place in the sea through millions upon millions of years of evolution. It plays an essential role as the top predator in the food web, culling out the weak so the strong may survive. As Stewart Springer, a noted shark researcher, once observed:

. . . sharks occupy in the sea somewhat the same position that man occupies on land; neither is particularly endangered except by others of its kind.

PETER C. HOWORTH

The day is beginning to dawn when humans are viewing sharks not as malefactors, but as benefactors which deserve their place on our watery planet.

Inside back cover: The color pattern of the blue shark makes it difficult to spot. Photo by Marty Synderman

Back cover: Divers seize a tiger shark in the South Pacific. Photo by Al Giddings-Ocean Images.

Other books on marine life: Big Sur, Biscayne, Channel Islands, Santa Catalina—an Island Adventure, Whales Dolphins-Porpoises. By publishers of *The Story Behind the Scenery* books on National Parks.

KC Publications · Box 14429 · Las Vegas, NV 89114

Printed by Dong-A Printing and Publishing, Seoul, Korea
Color separations by Kedia/Kwangyangsa Co., Ltd